MONEY HACKS HANDBOOK

HOW TO TAKE CONTROL OF YOUR MONEY AND NOT GO BROKE

DRAGON FRUIT

MARIA LLORENS AND HUGO VILLABONA

FOREWORD BY DAVID CARLSON OF

Maria Llorens and Hugo Villabona/Mango Media, Inc.
2525 Ponce de Leon, Suite 300
Coral Gables, FL 33134
www.mangomedia.us

Publisher's Note: This is a work of humor with a hint of self-help.
The authors wish to thank all the experts, guides and experiences
which were considered during the writing process.

Money Hacks Handbook / Maria Llorens and Hugo Villabona. -- 1st ed.
ISBN 978-1-63353-117-8

DISCLAIMER

Money management can be complicated, but we've broken down the best and worst of it to make it as easy as can be. From your first checking account to buying your first home, we've got the information you need to make your money work. Our hacks don't shy away from the nitty gritty of credit reports, loans, and saving for your life's dreams.

If you're confused about what to do with your money—this guide is for you. We've tried to get every perspective on money advice. Everyone needs to make their money work for them, and there are plenty of ways to avoid the black whole of bad credit and empty pockets. We can't give you a million dollars, but we can give you the tools that might get you a million in that retirement account someday. Hey, it's something. Whether your goal is just to get by with your cash or to become a billionaire, we've got a hack for it.

"It's all about the Benjamins."

- Puff Daddy

CONTENTS

CONTENTS   06
FOREWORD   09

CHAPTER 1 // Money on Your Mind   13

What Are You Worth?   15
Accounting Your Accounts   19
Making a Budget   25
Credit and Debt   29
Types of Credit   37

CHAPTER 2 // Spend, Spend, Spend   45

The Necessities   47
Transportation   55
Going Out   59
Fashion Finances   63
Tech Tools   67

CHAPTER 3 // How You Lose Money   71

Treat Yo Self   73
Uh Oh, Taxes   77
Identity Theft and Credit Card Fraud   83
Common Scams   89

CHAPTER 4 // Big Moves   93

Moving to a New City   95
Education   99
Self-Employment/Freelance   103
Starting a Business   107
Around the World   111

CHAPTER 5 // Planning for the Future   **115**

Buying a House   117
Marriage and Partnership   123
Your Kid, Your Cat, and Your Mom   127
Retirement   131

SOURCES   **136**

FOREWORD

When I graduated college five years ago I stumbled into the transition of the "real world" that millions of graduates make each year. At that time there was a seemingly endless number of decisions to be made surrounding my finances. They included how much money to save and how much to put towards student loans, where to live and how much to spend on rent, and how much to contribute to my retirement account.

On any given question related to my finances there were thousands of articles, books, and opinions to sift through. Information overload was an understatement.

After spending a lot of time over the past five years reading and learning about various personal finance topics my suggestion to 20-somethings is this: instead of attempting to master every personal finance topic, learn a little about a lot. For example you really don't need to know all the ins and outs of what goes into a credit score, but it can be helpful to understand why having a high credit score is important and how a credit score impacts your finances.

With the amount of content available about virtually any personal finance topic, many people struggle with the question of "where do I start?" That's where The Money Hacks Handbook comes into play. This book provides a solid base of information for anyone looking to gain a broad understanding of personal finance. With practical information and "hacks" on tons of topics from budgeting to credit cards, Money Hacks hits on all the important topics without overwhelming readers with unnecessary information. The information shared in this book will help you feel confident about your knowledge of finances – even if you feel lost right now.

If you are looking for a book that will provide you with an excellent overview of the personal finance topics that matter to you, I'm confident you will find the time you invest in reading this book to be highly profitable.

David Carlson
@davidcarlson1
YoungAdultMoney.com

Young Adult Money is a personal finance and lifestyle blog focused on helping those in their 20s and 30s to make more, save more, and live better.

CHAPTER 1 //
Money on Your Mind

Money on Your Mind //
What Are You Worth?

Before we get started, you'll need to take stock of your income. We're going to assume you either have a job or some other source of money (we won't tell anyone about your basement full of "money trees"). Your income and net worth, at least partially, determine your lifestyle and major decisions you'll make in the future.

Your net worth is basically your assets minus your debt. Do you have high credit card debt? What about student loans? It doesn't matter if your bank account has $20,000 in it (and if you're anything like us, it's more like $200), if your debt amounts to $40,000 you aren't worth much to begin with. In fact, you're worth negative dollars. Ouch.

It's okay, you have other good qualities.

On the semi-bright side, according to a 2014 Wall Street Journal article it only takes a net worth of $10,400 to be richer than most millennials. There's two ways to increase your net worth: pay off debt and increase your assets. We'll explain how to do each in more detail, but here are four simple things you can do right now:

Start an Emergency Fund

Simple, but difficult. You'll need to make sure your expenses are lower than your income, and that might mean cutting Thirsty Thursday from your social schedule. Your savings goals depend on your interests, but everyone needs an emergency fund. Aim to have three to six months' worth of your income in your savings.

Look to Make More Money

If your job isn't cutting it with the cash flow, figure out new ways to get your net worth out of the red. Whether it's negotiating for a higher salary or freelancing on the side, there are plenty of ways to keep your income from becoming stagnant.

Plan Your Loan Repayment

You gotta give back the money sometime. If you have federal loans, income-based repayment programs can make your payments dependent on salary. If you're not making much, maybe $20,000 a year, your payments can be as little as $0. If you have private loans, work with your lender to make a payment plan that fits your needs so you don't have to skimp on things that improve your life—like home ownership. Or an Xbox.

Prioritize

The whole point of having money is to pay for things that make your life better. So take stock of your interests and what really makes you happy. Is the latest iPhone the best way to spend those $200 dollars? Or would they be better spend on yoga classes or art supplies or a weekend get-away?

You're worth more than just numbers and dollar bills, but seeing as this is the way we've decided to structure society you may as well learn to take advantage of it. We here at Hacks Headquarters will be wishing for a Star Trek-like future where money seems to have just magically disappeared and everyone's just really into space and science and stuff.

WHAT IS A
GOOD CREDIT SCORE?

	MORTGAGE RATES	AUTO LOAN RATES	INSURANCE RATES	CREDIT CARD RATES
300-550 POOR CREDIT	**9.5%** Interest paid $259,000	**18.9%** Interest paid $13,828		**28.9%** Default Rate 75 %
550-620 SUBPRIME	**8.6%** Interest paid $229,000	**17.9%** Interest paid $13,009		**19.8%** Default Rate 50 %
620-680 ACCEPTABLE CREDIT	**4.9%** Interest paid $117,000	**11%** Interest paid $7,614		**13.9%** Default Rate 15-30 %
680-740 GOOD CREDIT	**4.2%** Interest paid $97,000	**6.5%** Interest paid $4,350		**12.4%** Default Rate 5%
740-850 EXCELLENT CREDIT	**3.9%** Interest paid $89,000	**5.1%** Interest paid $3,375		**7.99%** Default Rate 2 %

300-550 POOR CREDIT
Scores in this range may not be approved for a loan at all

550-620 SUBPRIME
The best thing one can do to improve a score is to pay down debts with on-time payments

620-680 ACCEPTABLE CREDIT
Rates in this range may vary widely

680-740 GOOD CREDIT
The medium score in the U.S. is 723

740-850 EXCELLENT CREDIT
Credit Scores will also affect things like employee background checks

Typical $160,000 loan with a 30-year Fixed mortgage

Typical 5-year auto loan of $25,000

Credit card rates will vary due to many different factors

Money on Your Mind //
Accounting Your Accounts

Y ou can't keep all your money in a tube sock in your drawer. I mean, you can, but it's weird and you'll be missing out on some sweet benefits of having a bank account. So drag your lazy butt over to the bank and get those accounts open to start spending (but mostly saving).

Checking Account

Your first bank account will likely be a checking account, which stores your money and offers easy access to it via a debit card and ATMs. You'll also get some checks with that account, which you should definitely keep around for the rare occasions where it's still needed. Those are the basics. Banks sometimes offer special packages and services, so make sure you're not getting anything you don't need. The most important thing about a checking account is to use it keep track of your balance and spending.

Money Hack – Overdraft Fees

So you lost track of your cash after buying too many Nicki Minaj songs on iTunes and now your account is in the negative. If you don't deposit money before your bank's cutoff time, you're going to get an overdraft fee. Ouch. If you do, you can sometimes talk your way out of the fee by calling or emailing your bank and explaining your situation. This may require a bit of lying, since they definitely will not care that you just had to listen to "Anaconda" commercial-free. Emphasize how you're a loyal customer and really appreciate their services and hopefully they'll take pity on you.

Savings Account

Once you get a job that pays more than just spending money, it's a good idea to start a savings account. You can just use a checking account, but it's not a good idea. You'll be more likely to spend it. Not only will your money be insured (up to $250,000), savings accounts also offer the ability for you to make a small amount of money as it earns interest.

Types of Savings Accounts

Basic:

 You will be able to withdraw money whenever you'd like and you will have a low minimum balance, but you won't earn much from interest (less than 1%).

Money Market:

 They pay more in interest, but will usually require a higher balance in the account at all times, and may restrict how many withdrawals you can make on a monthly basis.

Online Savings:

 You will handle these accounts solely on the internet or maybe over the phone, and they pay a higher interest rate. One caveat is it may take longer to access money from the account (a delay of a few days, even).

Certificates of Deposit (CD):

 A savings certificate entitling the owner to receive interest all at once when it's matured (instead of piecemeal like a bank account). Depending on the terms, a CD can pay higher rates than your standard bank account. The drawback is you won't be able to withdraw money whenever you'd like.w

Automatic Savings Plans:

 Here are 7 reasons why saving is good for you, and how to get into the habit early:

Save Small

Building a good habit is always a difficult task, so the best way to do it is to start small. Even if you're just saving an extra $1 every once in a while, it adds up and will feel less painful. Make a plan to save every time you get a paycheck—a hundred bucks here and there will make a big difference in time. Like exercise, it'll stop feeling terrible eventually.

Lifestyle Choices

Here's some bad news: your salary isn't really indicative of how much you can spend. It's really your salary after you pay bills, save, and establish an emergency fund that really shows what your spending money is. Keep that in mind every time your paycheck comes in and your first instinct is to hit the town.

Your Goals

What are your goals? Do you want to get married, buy a home, travel the world, write a novel, or some other big dream that requires not living paycheck-to-paycheck? Then save. You need money to turn those dreams into concrete realities. So save, live below your means (but still meeting your needs), and make your life wishes come true.

Emergency Fund

We mentioned this earlier, but don't stop at just one month's paycheck. Once you've established a minimum emergency fund, keep going. Employment is never a sure thing and you may need three months, six months, or a year's worth of paychecks to keep you afloat in tough times. The more you have saved, the more freedom and peace of mind you'll have when you're laid off or just want to take your life in a new direction.

Short-Term and Long-Term Savings

Little goals will help get you in the habit to save, so try saving up for something in the near-term that you want, like a vacation. While you're doing that, keep saving for your long-term goals—don't blow it all in one go. Stay organized by keeping a journal or other method of tracking how you're allocating your money.

Savings is Only One Goal

You may have other financial obligations, like paying credit card debt, student loans, or simply providing for your basic necessities. That's okay. Make sure to address the most urgent needs, and then get to saving. But don't forget about it entirely.

There are many reasons to stay on top of your checking and savings accounts, but the most important might be: financial independence. Whether it's from your parents, spouse or partner, credit card companies, or the government, having enough money to rely on means getting to call your own shots without wondering how you're going to pay for it all.

Money on Your Mind //
Making a Budget

Taking control of your money means not only knowing where to store and save it, but how to spend it. You've got a ton of bills to keep track of: food, rent, electricity, phone, internet, and more. And what's left over for having fun? Who can save when your minimum expenses take up your whole paycheck? How do you split that tiny paycheck when you can't get a raise? The 50/20/30 rule is a quick and easy way to keep your budget proportional.

50% -- The Essentials

Only 50% of your income should go to housing, transportation, food, and utilities. What portion of each category goes within that number depends on where you live. Maybe you're in a city with great public transportation, but the rent is sky-high. In that case, you can dedicate a little more money to rent and skip the car payments.

20% -- Financial Commitments

This category involves things that are secondary to necessities. You wouldn't be starving or homeless if you didn't pay for them. That would include credit card debt, savings deposits, retirement savings, and student loans, for instance. You still need to focus on these, because they affect you in the long term. Credit scores and savings, for instance, will affect your ability to buy a home. Start early with these savings and it'll earn interest for years to come.

30% -- Lifestyle Choices

This one is a bit up in the air, as it depends what you consider necessary and unnecessary. Do you need a phone? Probably. Maybe throw that back into "The Essentials." But do you need a cable plan with 400 channels? Not really. Consider that part of your discretionary spending.

Try to make your first priority in this category the essentials of what makes you happy and mentally sound, rather than on material things you don't need: your yoga classes, grabbing drinks with friends, or some toys for your dog.

Budget Tips

The Hard Line.

 Think of your budget as a guideline, not a rule. Just don't go overboard.

Invest.

 If you have enough, consider spending 5-10% of your pay on your 401(k) and maybe a Roth IRA. We'll discuss both later, so keep it in mind.

Self-Awareness.

 If you know you can't live without that grande mocha latte or whatever every morning, include it in your budget, and cut somewhere else. Don't let your impulses derail your budget.

First Things First.

 Pay your bills as soon as you're paid, even if it's before the due date. You'll avoid spending what you don't have, and you'll have a clearer picture of what you can spend for fun.

Free Fun.

 Don't think that you can only have fun with money, just make an extra effort to find free, cool things to do. Chances are your friends are in the same boat, and wouldn't mind an outing on the cheaper side.

Think Ahead.

 Remember anything can happen, so save for emergencies and don't skimp on maintenance for yourself or your stuff. That may mean springing for healthcare or getting new tires for your car. Remember that in the long run, going without those things will cost you more, and could possibly be dangerous.

If you find that you can't make ends meet with these guidelines, then the problem may be your income. Ask for a raise, get a new job, call up mom and dad, or take on freelance projects for extra cash. Don't settle for a salary that makes you stressed and doesn't meet your necessities and financial goals.

**Money on Your Mind //
Credit and Debt**

The major thing to understand is that credit isn't free money. The money you spend on a card or loan is called a balance, and the company giving it you credit is charging you a fee on that balance: interest. You can avoid interest by paying off your balance every month. If you don't, interest will add up every day or every month, depending on how the bank calculates the charges. You'll end up paying more in the long run for your purchases, but it can be worth it for a big and necessary purchase. Think computers and cars—not your groceries.

Why Credit?

You may be tempted to avoid the credit business altogether, and it'd be hard to blame you for the inclination. The average American household has over $15,000 in credit card debt and over $32,000 in student loan debt. That's a scary prospect, but the former is avoidable if you're smart about credit. Less avoidable are student loans, but we'll get into that in the next section.

There are several good reasons credit can be good for you. In general, it's something you may rely on when making a big financial decision or life change. Maybe you're moving to a new city and need to rent a decent apartment—they're likely to look at your credit history. Or if you want to buy a house or start a business, good credit is fundamental to being approved for those big loans.

Your Credit Score

Your credit score is a three-digit number calculated from your credit history. It ranges from 300 to 850. The graphic below shows what counts as a good rating, and what doesn't. Your score will affect whether you can get a loan or a credit card, and if you can, will affect how high of an interest rate you'll get.

Smart Credit Habits

Here are a few ways to take advantage of credit early on, so it doesn't hurt you in the long run:

Monitor Your Credit.

It's important to keep track of how financial actions affect your credit score. Simply applying for more than a few cards can result in a few points going down. There are many free and paid services that allow you to keep track of your score, and everyone is guaranteed a free credit report once a year. Some cards, like Discover, come with free online banking and give you a free credit score as part of the service.

Pay Your Bills.

This doesn't apply solely to your credit card payment every month, though that is a major way to keep your score up. Whether it's hospital bills, cell phone bills, or rent, all of it affects your credit score. Anything that goes unpaid goes to collections, a big stain on your credit report that won't go away for several years.

Pay Above the Minimum.

Paying as much off as you can every month, not just the minimum payment. It shows creditors you're reliable and they're more likely to raise your credit limit after a few months.

Keep Your Balance Low.

High balances on all of your credit cards will negatively impact your credit score. It doesn't matter if you're paying on time, having a lot of debt will knock down your score a few points. Pay them off and control your spending.

Remember Your Student Loans.

Even though it's pretty much expected for students to have loan debt at this point, it still affects your ability to get credit or future loans. Start paying them off as soon as you can, even if it's only a few bucks at a time.

If you're starting your credit history with a clean slate or you're still building credit, congrats! It's something you only get to do once, so be careful. It's much easier to ruin your credit than it is to fix it. Even if you've already made a few mistakes, with these tips in mind you should be able to get back on track soon enough.

CREDIT CARD TERMINOLOGY

ANNUAL FEE

The once-a-year cost of owning a credit card. Some credit card providers offer cards with no annual fees. The annual fee is part of the total cost of credit.

ANNUAL PERCENTAGE RATE (APR)

The yearly interest rate charged on outstanding credit card balances.

BALANCE

An amount of money. In personal banking, balance refers to the amount of money in a savings or checking account. In credit, balance refers to an amount of money owed.

CREDIT BUREAU

A reporting agency that collects information on consumer credit usage. There are currently three main credit bureaus in the United States: Equifax, Experian, and Trans Union.

CREDIT LINE

The maximum dollar amount that can be charged on a specific credit card account.

CREDIT RATING

A financial institution's evaluation of an individual's ability to manage debt. It is necessary to have a good credit rating if you intend to borrow money or have credit cards.

GRACE PERIOD

The time a borrower is allowed after a payment is due to make that payment without adding to the interest owed.

INTRODUCTORY RATE

Credit card issuers may offer low introductory annual percentage rates as special promotions. Be sure to fully understand how long the introductory rate will last and what the standard rate will be.

MINIMUM PAYMENT

The lowest amount of money that you are required to pay on your credit card statement each month in order to keep the account in good standing.

OVERDRAFT PROTECTION

A banking service that allows you to link your checking account to your credit card, thereby protecting you from overdraft penalties or bounced checks in the case of insufficient funds.

CREDIT REPORT

your complete credit history

ACCOUNT INFORMATION

a complete list of all credit accounts and thier status at the time the information was reported by your lenders and creditors

INQUIRES

companies that have requested your credit file for marketing purposes (as permitted by law), for a periodic review of your credit, and /or to consider extending credit or granting a loan

❌ NEGATIVE INFORMATION

accounts that contain a negative status

① COLLECTIONS

accounts that your lenders and/or creditors have turned over to a collection agency

② PUBLIC RECORDS

includes items obtained from local, state and federal courts, such as bankruptcies, liens and judgements

PERSONAL INFORMATION

identification information including your name, social security number, date of birth, address information and employment information

DISPUTE FILE INFORMATION

how to dispute information found on your credit report

PRINT CREDIT REPORT

print out your complete Credit Report for future reference

TIPS ON FIXING
CREDIT REPORT ERRORS

- Review all 3 credit reports

- Start your dispute with the credit bureau

- Contact the creditor too

- Monitor credit reports for even minor errors

- Maintain records of the dispute

- Be patient

- Consider a lawyer

You can get **1 report** from each of the 3 main bureaus for **free once per year** at: **AnnualCreditReport.com**

If you can't get your errors resolved & they're hurting your financial life, **consider a lawyer.**

Use the National Association of Consumer Advocates at: **naca.net**

**Money on Your Mind //
Types of Credit**

C redit is a big topic, so it's good to know what kinds of credit exist and how each will benefit you (or not). How many cards should you have? How often should you get new credit? Asking these beginner questions will help you avoid making huge mistakes down the line.

Types of Accounts

Revolving.

A revolving credit line involves making payments each month, with the payment depending on how much of the credit line you've used. You'll be charged interest for everything you don't pay off within a month. Credit cards and home equity credit are two examples.

Installment.

An installment account has a fixed payment every month and the total sum of the loan must be paid back over a set period of time (usually several years). A set amount of interest is charged over that time. Car loans, mortgages, student loans, business loans, personal loans, and home equity loans all fall under this category.

Open.

Open accounts need to be paid off in full each month. No interest and no installment payments are involved. Your cell phone and electric bills, for example, are open accounts.

How Much Credit?

There's no sure-fire ratio for how much credit and what variety of credit you should have. In general, it's good to have both revolving and installment accounts. You'll usually have open accounts anyway, but they aren't always reported to credit bureaus. Just pay those on time and you should be all right.

The thing to watch out for is too many credit cards. One or two installment loans are a sign of a responsible borrower since you're making steady payments over a long period of time. You can have more than a few cards, but you'll need to keep your balances low to justify it.

Credit Impact

 Take note that opening, maintaining, and closing accounts will all affect your credit score. Sometimes it's better to keep an account open and unused than to close it, for instance.

Balances.

 If you have several credit cards, give each one room to breathe. You don't want to max out any one card—spread it out over several, always keeping in mind what you can actually afford.

Hard Inquiries.

 This is the "hard pull" we talked about earlier. Watch your timing on asking for new credit. A bunch of accounts opened at the same time (or even just trying to open them) suggests you're a little desperate for money, and will affect your score when each company pulls your credit history to judge whether to approve you.

On-time Payment.

 Your payment history is a huge factor in keeping a good credit score. Don't be late!

Closing Accounts.

 Oddly enough, paying off all of your loans or closing excess credit cards may cause a dip in your credit score. Should you put off repayment? Maybe not. Your credit score isn't the only part of your financial health that you should consider. Think about how the loan limits you in other ways.

Credit Report Tips

 Your credit report is a vital way to prevent fraud and keep track of your credit health. You get a free one every year from Experian, Equifax, and Transunion, so use it! For more info on reading your credit report, refer to the graphics after this section.

Know the Basics.

No every lender sends reports to every bureau. You could have an account on one credit bureau that isn't listed on another. Make sure to check all three.

Check for Accuracy.

An error on your report can be a big hit to your credit score. There is always the possibility of fraud as well. You can dispute the mistake, but you'll usually need documentation as proof. Check that your payment history and accounts, especially credit cards, are all in order.

Debt-to-Credit Ratio.

Take note if your ratio is too high. It means you have more debt than available credit, and it's not good for your long-term financial plans, like a mortgage. Keep it less than 50%, preferably in the 30s.

Information Removal.

Collections and public records of foreclosures and bankruptcies will stay on your credit report for 7-10 years. Make sure they haven't been on there longer than that.

Credit can be overwhelming, and you may even want to opt out of the whole mess altogether. The most important thing is to not go past your means. Keep track of your spending and check your credit report regularly, and you should be fine.

CREDIT, DEBIT, OR CASH?

CREDIT CARD

PROS

Can help build credit. Your credit card use is typically reported to the bureaus that maintain your credit history, so establishing a good record of timely payments and keeping your balances at a modest level are great ways to build a healthy credit score.

Opportunity to earn rewards. One of the main reasons consumers like credit cards is because many offer rewards for using them like cash back, airline miles, sign-up bonuses and more. For those who pay their cards off in full each month (and never pay interest), these rewards can feel like getting paid to shop.

Security. Credit cards typically offer stronger protection against fraudulent charges than debit cards. Thanks to the Fair Credit Billing Act, you're only liable for unauthorized purchases up to $50-- and many issuers may not hold you accountable for those charges at all. A stolen credit card doesn't lead someone directly to the cash in your bank accounts either.

Insurances, warranty plans and other perks. To vie for your business, credit card companies often offer additional benefits. From auto rental insurance to price protection to warranties on big-ticket items, these little-known benefits are definitely advantages that credit cards might offer over other payment methods.

CONS

Temptation to spend. Credit cards may not be the best option for those with shopping addictions or those who may feel the need to use their cards just because the credit is available to them. However, if you make a conscious effort to use your credit card like a debit card by not spending money that you don't have, you may be able to minimize your debt load.

May negatively affect credit health. Both good and bad payment history can be reported to the credit bureaus, so mistakes like over-utilizing your card, not using your card at all and paying late can hurt your credit health.

Can be expensive to use. Credit cards may come with late fees, annual fees and a variety of other charges, including interest if you don't pay your balance in full. Be sure you understand the terms of each of your cards, as they can be complicated.

DEBIT CARD

PROS

Easier to control expenses and avoid overspending. Because you're using your own money from your checking account to pay for your purchases (unless you overdraft), debit cards can feel more like "real money" and may help you control your spending. Compared to cash, it can also be an easier way to keep track of where your money is going-- just log into your online banking account and view your recent activity.

Generally cheaper to get cash quickly. Unlike with credit cards, there's usually no need for a (potentially costly) cash advance fee. Using a debit card, all you generally need to do is find your bank's nearest ATM or ask for cash back with your purchases. Of course, you may also need to pay fees to get cash using a debit card in some situations, like when you use an out-of-network ATM.

Some security. While the protections may not be as strong as with credit cards, the Electronic Fund Transfer Act limits your liability for unauthorized charges on a debit card depending on when you report the debit card as lost or stolen.

Better exchange rate on foreign currency. While credit cards generally offer better protections against theft for those traveling abroad, debit cards may offer better rates if you need foreign currency. According to Lifehacker, when you use your debit card and hit the ATM, "you generally get the 'wholesale' exchange rate, which is reserved for interbank purchases, and superior to the exchange rate you'd get on your account statement if you just swiped your plastic."

CONS

Few (or no) rewards. Debit cards don't usually come with cash back, price protection and other perks that credit cards offer. In most cases, you simply pay for your purchase without getting anything back.

Overdraft fees. If you're not careful, you may spend more money than you have in your checking account and incur an overdraft fee. However, some lenders allow you to set up alerts to notify you by text or email when your balance is low, making fees easier to avoid. You can also set up account alerts through Credit Karma if you link an online financial account to your Credit Karma account and set up your monitoring preferences.

CASH

PROS

Universally accepted offline. While some businesses only accept cash, you won't find many that only accept credit or debit cards. Paper money is the surest way to purchase small ticket items.

Everyone can use it. In order to get a credit card, you need to apply for one and risk being denied. Even some checking accounts (and the debit cards linked to those accounts) may be hard to get if a consumer has a limited banking history or insufficient identification. With cash, you never have to worry about any of those issues.

Easy to avoid overspending. With cash, once you run out, you can't use it to buy anything until you get more. Relying on cash can be a good way to ensure you live within your means.

CONS

Can't use online. Many popular retailers like Amazon and eBay exist primarily online and require electronic payments-- if a product is only sold on an online site, you can't go to a physical store to buy it with cash.

Doesn't establish credit history. Sometimes you may need to prove your creditworthiness to get what you want, such as when you're applying for that dream apartment rental. If you've only been making purchases with cash, you may run into some difficulties qualifying because cash purchases aren't reported to the credit bureaus.

Can't be replaced if stolen. While many credit and debit cards have systems in place to offset fraudulent activity, there's usually no way to prove that your cash was yours. Once it's gone, it's probably gone.

CHAPTER 2 //
SPEND, SPEND, SPEND

**Spend, Spend, Spend //
The Necessities**

How much should you be spending on rent, food, your phone, and all the other necessities of adult life? Well, ideally as little as possible. But we know that's not always the case, so we're going to help you navigate the tricky waters of expensive apartments and ramen noodles.

Getting Your Own Place

That title is kind of misleading, because we're going to suggest you do the opposite. We know, after all those years of living away from your parents, you'd think you could continue the sweet trend of living on your own. But that's unlikely to be possible in a major city right away unless you've got some money saved up or a job lined up with a killer salary. Here are some tips for figuring out your housing situation in the first few years.

Live with Your Parents.

 The whole point of this option is to save money. If your parents happen to live in a city where you can work and not be miserable, do it. Build a nest egg for your big move, whether it's to your own place or another city.

Avoid Hip Neighborhoods.

 When you do finally start looking for a place that isn't your parents' house, go for a neighborhood that is safe, but not trendy. Aim for up-and-coming or family friendly vs. well known.

Find Roommates.

 Rents in major cities start at around $1,000. Start. So it's likely you're going to have to find a good roommate (or two, or three) to share an apartment or house. Give yourself some time to find a good roommate, maybe a month or two. Friends, friends of friends, Craigslist. The most important thing is to think ahead about what qualities you want in a roommate. And maybe do a background check.

Pick the Right Space.

 Private bedrooms where everyone can retreat to when they don't want to interact are your best bet, but find an apartment that suits your lifestyle. Don't get into a situation that's going to make you miserable.

Get it in Writing.

 If you have a shared lease, for instance, get a standard contract online and ask your roommate to fill it out to guarantee what share of the rent is theirs. Add any other terms that you think are reasonable, like utility payments.

Be Straightforward.

 Set up ground rules for living with your roommate and hold them to it. No one likes a perpetually dirty bathroom.

Take Advantage of Roomies.

 Roommates don't have to be a huge burden. They can be a great social resource and will keep loneliness at bay when you're new to a big city.

Food, Face it:

We all love to eat. We'd like to think if money was short we'd just tough it out with ramen noodles and water, but that's not true. You'd rather hit up that dollar menu three times a day and possibly need major heart surgery at 30 than eat than eat soft noodles and salt. The truth is, if you make a livable salary, in the $30k range or higher, you can afford some decent food.

Spend Less on Groceries

The main takeaways for spending less on food are: eat out less and don't waste food. Yes, this may involve some cooking on your part, but you were going to have to learn how to do that eventually. Here are a few tips for saving at the supermarket:

Make a Plan.

Reflect on your eating habits and make a plan around them. Do you always need an afternoon snack and three meals a day? Shop for it. Next, decide what you want to eat each week. Take advantage of leftovers, too.

Decide what to Eat.

Planning your meals ahead of time sounds like a chore. If you know you'll have a craving for pizza at some point, budget that into your plan or pick a cheaper option, like frozen pizza.

Stock Up.

The best way to avoid needing to eat out is by keeping plenty of non-perishable ingredients available at home. Think pasta, canned veggies and beans, and olive oil. If your refrigerator has more than condiments and chocolate pudding in it, you don't have an excuse.

Stay in Season.

Check out our handy chart for a quick guide on when certain veggies and fruits are in season (and at their cheapest). Don't bother making kale smoothies in the summer—you'll end up paying more.

Shopping List.

Write a list and stick to it based on what you've decided to eat, that way you won't be buying things you don't need. You'll always have weekly staples— milk, bread, eggs—but beyond that you'll need a plan.

Clip, Clip.

Coupons may sound like your grandma's fare, but who better than that penny-pincher to know about saving money? Don't, however, clip coupons for things you don't need that week.

Down to the Club.

Club stores, that is. Costco and Sam's Club have great discounts on mass amounts of necessary items like toilet paper. You'll spend more upfront, but in the long run you'll save. Also stock up on those non-perishables.

Shop Ethnic Stores.

 Ethnic stores often have tasty ingredients at cheaper prices than your usual supermarket. It's a good way to liven up your menu without breaking the bank.

Farm the Farm.

 Farmers' markets may not be your best bet with finding cheap produce, but pick-your-own farms can get you a better deal.

Cut the Meat.

 Meat in your food budget is usually not nice to your wallet. Aim for a few vegetarian meals each week. You'll be helping the environment and your expenses.

Your Phone

What else takes a big chunk out of your "necessities" budget? That little device you use to tap away at Tweets and ignore emails from work. We're going to call this one a necessity since, c'mon, who uses a landline anymore? Here area few tips for cutting that annoying bill:

Avoid Frequent Upgrade Plans.

Upgrade offers like AT&T Next seem like a bargain— you pay monthly installments on a phone for a set amount of months, then switch to a new phone. Usually you'll be paying half of the retail price. But **a)** you can't keep the old phone and **b)** if you have a contract, you'll usually pay more than if you just pay the upgrade fee upfront. That's usually $200 plus tax for an iPhone vs. 18 months of $22 installments— nearly $400 dollars.

Check Your Bill.

It's convenient to set up auto-pay, but you may get an extra charge or two on there if you don't keep an eye on the bill. You may also be using less texts and data than what you're paying for. Talk to your company about other, cheaper plans.

Skip Insurance.

The value of a brand new phone decreases significantly after 6-12 months, so paying $10-$15 extra per month for insurance becomes less reasonable too. Cut the insurance as you get closer to your next upgrade.

Consider going Small.

Smaller carriers often use the same coverage as larger companies, so don't shy away from their month-to-month plans. The big carriers can get you tied up in long contracts and outdated equipment.

Use Skype More.

Skype is free, so take advantage of it using a Wi-Fi connection for your calls.

Get on the Family Plan.

Family plans will often help you save money and get better data limits, for instance. Just ask your folks if you can pay your share and you're good to go.

Don't let even the necessities take over your budget. There are plenty of ways of cutting costs, but it does take a little extra effort. Don't shy away from planning ahead for those everyday purchases—the price tag isn't inevitable.

THE EAT SEASONABLY CALENDAR

FRUITS & VEGETABLES

 Apple Bramly

 Apple Cox

 Asparagus

 Beans Broad

 Beans Runner

 Blackberry

 Blueberry

 Brussel

 Cabbage Green

 Cabbage White

 Cabbage Savoy

 Cabbage Red

 Carrot

 Cauliflower

 Celery

 Cucumber

 Cherry

 Courgette

 Kale

 Leeks

 Lettuce Cos

 Marrow

 Letuce Iceberg

 Lettuce Curly

 Peas

 Plum

 Potatoes Maincrop

 Raspberry

 Rhubarb

 Spinach

 Sweetcorn

 Strawberry

 Squash

WINTER

December

January

February

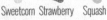

SPRING

March

April

May

FRUITS & VEGETABLES

 Apple Bramly

 Apple Cox

 Asparagus

 Beans Broad

 Beans Runner

 Blackberry

 Blueberry

 Brussel

 Cabbage Green

 Cabbage White

 Cabbage Savoy

 Cabbage Red

 Carrot

 Cauliflower

 Celery

 Cucumber

 Cherry

 Courgette

 Kale

 Leeks

 Lettuce Cos

 Marrow

 Letuce Iceberg

Lettuce Curly

 Peas

 Plum

 Potatoes Maincrop

 Raspberry

 Rhubarb

 Spinach

 Sweetcorn

 Strawberry

 Squash

SUMMER

June

July

August

FALL

September

October

November

**Spend, Spend, Spend //
Transportation**

You need to get around town somehow, but the cost of a car seems overwhelming. Between repairs, maintenance, insurance, and gas, you may as well cut your losses and walk everywhere. There are several options for transportation saving, so consider each one before you commit to your own vehicle.

Buy, don't Lease.

You may be tempted to get a shiny new car, especially after graduation, but it's a bad idea. It's much safer and cheaper to find a used car in good shape. Look on Craigslist, Autotrader, Cars.com, and other sites to find your next ride.

Finance, don't Lease.

At the end of a lease, you end up with another lease for a different car. You don't own anything. If you can't afford to buy a car outright, save up for a down payment and finance the car instead. You'll end up with a car at the end of that, and it's all yours to sell in the future.

Shop Around for Gas.

Gas prices vary by station, and there are apps like GasBuddy that help you find the cheapest one.

Carpool.

If you have a car, consider charging your co-workers a bit of gas money to be their driver. Or ask them if you can tag along in the morning.

Consider Sharing.

There are plenty of ride and car sharing companies now, like Zipcar and Uber. If you're not making a big commute every day, consider skipping the car and using sharing services when you need to do groceries or get across town.

Public Transportation.

If it's feasible where you live, buy that subway or bus pass and get yourself around town with your fellow commuters. Enjoy being driven around and take a book with you.

Buy Online.

One of our main uses for a car is lugging home the stuff we bought at the grocery store or IKEA. Skip the big buying spree and do it online instead. You can buy coffee, a mug, and a coffee table all on Amazon. No need to leave the house.

Walk.

Get your body moving! If the weather is nice and your destination is nearby, walking is a free as it gets.

Bike.

Take care to follow road rules, wear a helmet, and watch out for drivers in a hurry, but biking is a great way to get to nearby places quickly. And it's much better for you than a stressful drive to work.

Ask a Friend.

If you and your friends are going out together, or you're on their way home, ask for a ride. Don't be shy, just be considerate.

These hacks will definitely help you save on getting around town, and they're probably most effective when combined. Chances are you may need to own a car, but keep those maintenance and gas costs down by walking and biking more, for instance. See what works for you, and never settle for less than keeping your costs down and helping the environment a bit too.

**Spend, Spend, Spend //
Going Out**

Y ou're out on the town with friends, and then you suddenly feel faint after looking at the drink bill. Those craft beers add up, kiddo. You can always just stay home and never have fun, but who wants to do that? Your social activities will probably have the biggest impact on your bill, so it's worth it to rein them in. Here are some ways to stay within your budget and still get to enjoy your evenings out.

Be the Planner.

This is the best way to take control of how your evenings go. Be the person who always plans the evening among friends. If not, don't be passive about where you want to go and how much you want to spend. When someone else suggests a place that might be out of your range, throw in your own suggestion.

Look for Alternatives.

Fix your social calendar so it has less expensive nights out and more frugal fun evenings. Instead of going out to a bar, maybe throw a house party with a few beers. Instead of a concert with a $100 ticket, go to a local show of an up-and-coming band. There are endless options for keeping things fun and cheap.

Plan Ahead.

Impulsive outings are fun, but sometimes a wallet-killer. Plan your outings ahead of time to look for the best deal, especially on vacations or weekend getaways.

Have Pre-Drinks.

It's the age-old trick. Stock up on something cheaper from the supermarket, get a couple drinks in you, and then only buy one or two when you hit the bar.

Have a Good Meal.

Eating before you go out won't only curb the bad hangover you're building up to, but it'll also be easier on your budget than a full meal and drinks.

Leave the Card at Home.

You'll be tempted to spend more. And when you want to get cash out, use your bank's ATM, not the one at the club.

Always be on the lookout for fun and free things to do in your city. It's much better than going to the same bars every weekend, and it'll be easier on your cash.

Spend, Spend, Spend //
Fashion Finances

We've all got to wear clothes, unfortunately, and you don't want to look like you picked them out of the trash (unless you do want that hobo chic look). Clothes are cheaper than ever, but sometimes we buy too many of them. We're drawn in by those 50% off sales and "buy one get one" offers and we can't resist having 5 shirts in the same color. Well, hackers, we're going to put those clothing habits to rest.

Dress for Less

Sell Old Clothes.

If last season's blouse just doesn't cut it anymore, drop it off at a consignment shop. The store will sell your clothing, then give you a portion of the sale. If you haven't worn something in at least a year, it's got to go.

Thrift Stores.

Thrift stores will sell used clothes at a deep discount; just make sure to wash them. Watch out for vintage stores, though. They sell trendy retro pieces at steep prices because they're rare.

Coupons.

Yep, they're back. Your trusty friends made of paper and barcodes. Don't just walk into the mall without having checked if your favorite store is offering a discount if you print their coupon before you walk in.

Know What to Buy.

Walking into the mall without a plan is exactly what stores want you to do. Impulse buys are going to rack up your clothing expenses. Avoid them by making a list of what you actually need and make sure it goes with your wardrobe.

Avoid Dry Cleaning.

Clothes that need to be dry-cleaned should be saved for special occasions only. You'll end up paying more in the long run to care for high maintenance fabrics.

Care for Your Clothes.

Not having to buy new clothes is the best way to avoid spending too much. Don't use harsh settings on the washer and don't use one item too frequently.

Don't Sweat on It.

For reasons we have yet to understand, workout clothes can be ridiculously expensive. Sure they look nice, but are you going to burn any more calories in that than an old t shirt? Save money and borrow your brother's old basketball shorts.

Rent for Events.

If you're only going to need that fancy dress for an evening, consider renting. Services like Rent the Runway and Gwynnie Bee offer rental or subscription services for clothes.

Get Simple for Cheap.

If you're looking for a basic polo or tank for layering, avoid designer brands. A white tank from Old Navy or Walmart looks about the same as a more expensive one. If you're just going to wear it under something else, go cheap.

Skip the Sale.

If you're not going to wear it, don't buy it. Even if it "only" costs five dollars. It's money that could go to something else.

Americans spend an average of $1,700 dollars a year on clothing and accessories, according to the Christian Science Monitor. Don't get caught up in that habit, that money could be used for a vacation, car payments, or even delicious food. All of those are more valuable than another pair of expensive jeans.

**Spend, Spend, Spend //
Tech Tools**

Since you've probably got your face stuck in a phone half the time anyway, you may as well take advantage of what technology has to offer. There are a ton of apps for iOS and Android that help you save money or just keep track of it, so here are some of the best:

Mint.

With Mint, you'll input all your accounts—checking, savings, retirement, credit cards, even student loans. Every transaction is recorded, and once Mint analyzes your spending habits, you'll get alerts on unusual expenses or a low bank balance. It creates a budget for you and gives advice on where to best put your money (pay of card "x" first, leave debt on card "y").

BillTracker.

Keep all of your bill notifications in one place, along with amounts and due dates. There's also a calendar view and it allows password protection.

Shopkick.

Shopkick helps you browse products from stores like Target, Macy's, Best Buy and more. You can discover great deals and earn points when you make purchases or even by walking into the stores. Point are then transferred into gift certificates.

Ibotta.

We like money, you like money, and we especially like free money. Ibotta lets you earn money for shopping by complet-ing tasks—like watching a video, taking a poll, or sharing a post on Facebook—cash is added to your account. It can be accessed once you purchase a product from one of the 50 retailers partnered with Ibotta. When the purchase is verified, cash is put into your PayPal account or into gift cards.

RetailMeNot.

The app based on the desktop site has thousands of coupons from nearly every store you can think of, both for online and in-store shopping. Search for deals at nearby stores and save the coupons you like. No more printing coupons, just show it at the register.

SnipSnap.

If you still get print coupons in the mail, digitize them with SnipSnap. Take photos of the ones you need and just show them at the register in-store.

Grocery IQ.

Make your shopping list digital with this grocery list app. Build your list with specific brands and items with the app's database, or use voice recognition and barcode scanning. The app also offers coupons.

Groupon.

Use Groupon to find deals for local restaurants, beauty salons, yoga classes, and tons more. They also have Groupons for products or even vacations. The service is consistently good, especially for 2-for-1 outings.

DebtTracker Pro.

If you've made some financial mistakes in the pass, go for this app. It creates a payoff plan and visualizes your debt for you. You'll know if you've spent 30% or 80% of your credit on a certain card. It recommends payment strategies and sends reminders when payments are due. The best way to get out of debt is to know how badly you're in it.

Viggle.

Money for watching TV? It's what we've always dreamed of! Viggle lets users "check in" to whatever show they're watching and earn points that can be redeemed at various stores. Earn additional points by playing games and testing your TV IQ.

There are a ton more apps out there than just these 10, but between Mint and Groupon alone you'll start to see a big difference in your spending. Put that phone time to use and stay in control of your finances by spending less (without losing out on fun) and knowing the full picture of your finances on-the-go.

CHAPTER 3 //
How You Lose Money

How To Lose Money //
Treat Yo Self

We've talked about necessities, but sometimes it's good to buy something you either don't completely need or is useful but happens to be shiny. Extra shiny. In that case, you need a strategy for those big purchases. You want to avoid the mistake of getting saddled with debt over something that isn't all that important, but you also want to have fun once in a while.

How to Buy Big

Save for It.

 We know, it's the most boring way to get things done money-wise, but it pays off and it won't cost you extra the way putting it on credit will.

How to do It:

i. Easy. First, count up how many paychecks you're getting between now and when you want purchase.

ii. Divide the total cost of the purchase by the number of paychecks.

iii. Voila! You have your savings amount. If you can't afford to save that much in time for the purchase, then you need to set your goal date a little further along. Or cut from your usual budget to save money.

Evaluate Your Desire.

 What's the point of this purchase? Are you an artist eyeing a brand new digital tablet or are you just in the mood for a fancy new 3D TV? The first option may be something that improves your work and makes you happy, while the latter is merely a passive entertainment item. It depends.

Opt for Experiences Instead.

 Most material things lose value over time, and have you ever noticed how they just seem to pile up, never to be used again? When thinking about ways money can enrich your life, opt for experiences. Psychologists say that an experience, like travel, has a longer lasting effect on your happiness than buying a material object. Ironically, even though your trip ends, it becomes a special memory. That "shiny, new" couch will eventually become that "old, ratty" cat scratcher.

Don't go for the card.

 Contrary to popular advice, it's better to use your card for small purchases that you easily pay off later. You'll earn more rewards that way and avoid the pains of interest. With a large purchase, you miss out on rewards and end up paying more in the long run.

Try used.

 A used or refurbished version of the item you want can save you money and probably work just as well. Sometimes people will return an opened, but new item, leaving you with an untouched item at a great price.

Consider another brand.

 Do you need the specific brand name version of the product you want, or does the second best brand work just as well? It may be hard to resist temptation, but pay for value, not a name.

Do Your research.

 Are the reviews good on the item? What problems will you run into? Will it need frequent maintenance or repairs? Consider all these things, some of which will cost you beyond the initial purchase.

It's not a bad thing to buy something fancy for yourself. In fact, you should reward yourself after hard work and saving up for a while. Just remember our advice, especially regarding experiences. Money isn't supposed to be a huge stress on your life or simply a source of material things. It can enrich your life depending on what you do with it.

**How You Lose Money //
Uh Oh, Taxes**

They come every year, and may be a pain or a pleasure depending on how you look at it. We're going for the latter, especially since everyone's favorite government related mail—tax returns—are the lovely reward you get after filing those pesky forms. Here's how to get the most out of those returns, even in your 20s.

Taxes and You

Claiming Allowances.

The first thing to think about with your tax return is maximizing how much money you can get back. Allowances make a portion of your income not count toward your taxes—money you get to keep. If you're single with no dependents, you should have at least one. If you had more than one job in the past year, you want to claim zero allowances on the lowest paying job, and one on the highest.

Deductions.

This is where you can really save, and inexperienced taxpayers usually miss a few. Here are some to remember next time you file:

    a. Student loan interest

    b. Certification fees

    c. Moving expenses

    d. Trade publication expenses

    e. Classroom expenses for teacher who pay for supplies out of pocket

    f. Tip-outs for those working in hospitality

Work from Home?

You can take a home office deduction, but you'll need to calculate how much of your house is your office. For example, if your office takes up 150 square feet, and your home is 1200 square feet, you can deduct 12% of all the utilities and maintenance of that apply to your home. Also, you can only include how much applies to the hours you've actually worked in there.

Work expenses.

Keep a record (receipts) of everything you do related to your job. Whether it's parking at a work event or drinks with a client, everything counts. Another tip: use your credit card company's spending graphs, if they offer them, to see how much you spent on things like restaurants and transportation.

Freelance = four.

If you're filling out a 1099 form, pay your taxes quarterly to avoid getting a big tax bill at the end of the year. Most online tax programs, like Intuit, can calculate it for you.

Get some help.

VITA, a volunteer tax assistant service, offers tax help to people earning under $53k a year for free. They usually work in libraries or universities. Find one in your area at this site: http://irs.treasury.gov/freetaxprep/

File it fast.

Taxes are due in April, but you can file them as early as January and get your return back by the end of the month if you choose to receive it via direct deposit.

Taxes don't have to be painful, so long as you know what to look for, or get help from someone who does. If you're really looking to save some dough, don't just gloss over the major parts of your return and call it a day. You could be missing out on a few hundred dollars or more from your return.

COMMON TAX FORMS

WHAT'S IN THE MAIL?

☑ **FORM W-2.** It's filled out by your employer to document your earnings for the calendar year. This tax form supplies you with some of the most important information you'll need when you fill out your **1040**, **1040A** or **1040EZ**, including the wages you earned and the taxes your employer withheld.

☑ **FORM 1098.** You'll receive one of the three varieties of this form if you paid interest on a mortgage or student loan, paid college tuition or donated a motor vehicle to charity.

☑ **FORM 1099 SERIES.** This family of tax forms reports all income that isn't salary, wages or tips. For example, you'll receive a 1099 if you earned more than $600 from any one company while working as an independent contractor, consultant or freelancer within the tax year. There are several types of 1099 forms, including:

✓ **1099-DIV**, which reports dividends, distributions, capital gains and federal income tax withheld from investment accounts, including mutual fund accounts.

✓ **1099-INT** keeps track of interest income you earn on investments.

✓ **1099-OID** (Original Issue Discount) is provided if you received more than the stated redemption price on maturing bonds.

✓ **1099-MISC** documents self-employment earnings, as well as miscellaneous income such as royalties, commissions or rents. It covers all non-employee income that is not derived from investments.

WHAT TO FILE?

☑ **FORM 1040EZ** is the simplest version of this essential tax form. You generally can file it if you:

✓ Have no dependents

✓ Are younger than **65**

✓ Earned less than **$100,000**

✓ Don't plan to itemize your deductions

☑ **FORM 1040A** is more comprehensive than **1040EZ**, but simpler than the regular **1040**. It lets you make certain adjustments to your taxable income, such as child tax credits or the deduction for stude nt-loan interest, but doesn't let you itemize deductions. You typically can use this form if you earn less than **$100,000** and don't have self-employment income.

☑ **FORM 1040** applies if the other two tax forms don't: for example, if you make **$100,000** or more, have self-employment income or plan to itemize deductions.

How You Lose Money //
Identity Theft and Credit Card Fraud

W ith so much of your personal information online these days, it's easier than ever to pretend to be someone else. Not to mention that very fallible human beings, who sometimes forget to blot out your social security number, handle your supposedly private information all the time. Add to that the very real possibility that your credit card information is easily subject to hackers' ill will, and you've got a situation ripe for identity theft. Here are a few ways to avoid

Avoiding Fraud

Monitor Your Bank and Credit Statements.

 Many banks and credit lenders automatically detect fraudulent behavior and lock your account, but still keep an eye out for fraudulent behavior on your statements every month, or every day with your online account.

Protect Your Passwords.

 Change logins and passwords every few weeks and don't use a debit card online. Your credit card has more protections if it's stolen. Make those passwords strong with at least eight characters, including a mix of letters, numbers, and symbols ($+r0^gh@h@).

Verify Your Address.

 Identity criminals may attempt to change your address with a change of address form at the post office, so that their fraudulent credit activity stays out of your mailbox. Give them a call and make sure everything is in order.

Eye Your Credit Report.

 Make sure all the accounts on your report and their respective amounts make sense and are yours. And be careful when getting your credit report, there are plenty of fake sites looking to steal your info. Only go to www.annualcreditreport.com each year for your free report.

Shred Your docs.

 Regularly shred outdated bank statements, credit card applications, bills, and another other documents with personal information before you throw it away. Even junk mail may have some personal information so shred those too.

Paid service.

 There are some services that protect against identity theft, but if you take the time to monitor your accounts yourself, they're largely unnecessary. And they can cost over $100 a year.

Your SSN.

 Don't carry your Social Security card in your wallet. If your health plan (other than Medicare) or another card uses your Social Security number, ask the company for a different number.

Be mysterious online.

 What you share on social networks (your home or email address; children's names; birth date and so on) is what tech-savvy thieves use for scams, phishing, and account theft.

Click with caution.

 When shopping online, check out a Web site before entering your credit card number or other personal information. Read the privacy policy and look for opportunities to opt out of information sharing. (If there is no privacy policy posted, shop elsewhere.) Only enter personal information on secure Web pages with "https" in the address bar and a padlock symbol at the bottom of the browser window. These are signs that your information will be encrypted or scrambled, protecting it from hackers.

It seems like a lot of work, but it's way more of a hassle to have someone steal your information. And your credit will take years to recover from a hit like that. Keep an eye on your loved ones' information when you can too—even kids are very likely to be targeted for credit fraud.

IDENTITY THEFT PROTECT YOURSELF

IT CAN HAPPEN IN AN INSTANT, EVERYONE IS AT RISK

ID THEFT WHO IS MOST AT RISK

1

Children are targeted 35 TIMES MORE often than adults

2

People with personal information on their social media profile

4

25% OF PEOPLE affected by fraud annually are dead people (Yes, dead)

3

SMARTPHONE owners have a **33% higher rate** of id fraud than that of general public

5

More often **COLLEGE STUDENTS** have good, clean credit scores, wich make them ideal targets.

6

Victims of data breaches **are 9.5 times more** likely to be a victim of ID fraud

7

HOUSEHOLDS WITH incomes greater than $150,000 are 7.7% more likely to be victimized

ID THEFT VICTIM PROFILE

 Every **3 SECONDS** someone's identity is stolen

Victims who found out about their identity theft more than 6 months after the fact incurred costs **FOUR TIMES** higher than the average

165 HOURS is the average amount of time victims spent repairing the damage donee by new fraduleent accounts

58 HOURS is the average amount of time victims spent repairing the damage donde to existing accounts

43 is the percentage of identity theft from stolen wallets, checkbooks, credit cards, billing statements, or other physical documents

ID THEFT FRAUD FACTS

In 2012, Identity Fraud **INCREASED BY 8%**

In the US more than **12.6 MILLION** Adults were Victims of Theft

62% of Smartphone Owners do not use a password on phone's home screen

32% of smartphone owners save Log-in ingformation on electtronic devices

Compared to 2010 there was a 67% increase in data breaches. The 3 most common items exposed are:

Credit card #   Debit card #   Social security #

**How You Lose Money //
Common Scams**

The world is full of scammers trying to steal your financial information, so keep an eye out and don't get suckered into common tricks. Along with the tips from the last section, make sure you learn to spot the most frequent offenders.

Scams, Phishing, and More

Telemarketing.

You may have gotten a call at some point that you've won a free gift, vacation, or prize. These were mostly likely schemes to get your personal or financial information, so don't ever fall for one, as convincing as it may sound. Here are some telltale signs:

    a. You must act 'now' or the offer won't be good."

    b. "You've won a 'free' gift, vacation, or prize." But you have to pay for "postage and handling" or other charges.

    c. "You must send money, give a credit card or bank account number

Nigerian Letter Fraud.

It seems laughable to many of us, but these emails are still circulating pretty frequently, and maybe an unsuspecting family member could be a target. Be proactive and send the letter to the US Secret Service or your local FBI office.

Ponzi Schemes.

Don't give money to strangers. Ponzi schemes promise high financial returns or dividends not available through traditional investments. Instead of investing the funds of victims, however, the con artist pays "dividends" to initial investors using the funds of subsequent investors.

Pyramid Schemes.

Pyramid schemes—also referred to as franchise fraud or chain referral schemes—are marketing and investment frauds in which an individual is offered a distributorship or

franchise to market a particular product. Basically, don't fall for someone who tells you to buy 100 cases of magical juice and recruit other people to sell that magical juice with you. 99% of Herbalife's investors lose money, according to Dr. Jon Taylor, a pyramid scheme scholar.

Craigslist Rent Scam.

The only thing that a landlord can legally ask you for before you see an apartment is your photo ID. After responding to an ad, it's common to get an email asking you to fill out a rental application and forward a credit report or score. If you do see this, stop contact immediately and report them to the FTC at this address: https://www.ftccomplaintassistant.gov /#crnt&panel1-1

Charities.

It's hard to think that that donation you made to a cancer research organization could be fake, but it's always possible. Charity fraud is common, but there are a lot of good resources to search for who's not being truthful. The Tampa Bay Times created a national database, so check it before you donate: http://charitysearch.apps.cironline.org/.

Work-at-Home Scams.

Many work-at-home ads that promise you can earn a great living are a scam too. Avoid Internet businesses, mystery shopping jobs, direct selling through a multilevel marketing plan or do your homework. Chances are someone's tried it and talked about it online.

Stay Updated.

The FTC updates their site with new scams regularly. Make sure to check them out once in awhile or do an internet search if you see suspicious behavior with your email, phone, or bank account.

We hate to think that people are out to get us, but easy money is tempting enough that there are many criminals attempting to steal your information. Be vigilant and suspicious when it comes to parting with your money. It's not a "Scrooge" thing to do, it's just common sense.

CHAPTER 4 //
Big Moves

Big Moves //
Moving to a New City

You're finally ready to move out, you know what to look for in housing, but what about everything else that goes into moving to a new place? It may seem like it's over after finding a job and a place to live, but there's a lot more to consider financially before and after you get there.

Saving While Moving

Choosing a city.

It's important to consider cost of living when choosing where to live. It varies widely from city to city. Use a cost of living calculator and think about your personal expenses. Whether you can make ends meet will affect your quality of life, so choose wisely.

Quality over quantity.

It may be that having to rough it for a few years is worth the life and opportunities you'll have in a particular place. Just make sure you have a good plan, some willpower to keep your budget in check, and some savings.

Job availability.

Think about where your industry is centered and look at joblessness rates in the cities you're considering. You don't want to make the job search more difficult than it is already. Ask around about how long it usually takes to find a job in your field and see whether you can support yourself in the meantime.

Take it easy.

A new city means new things to try, whether it's food, bars, events, and everything in between. Don't go nuts, though, trying all the city has to offer in a week. Give yourself some time, maybe a month or so, to really see how your budget holds up to your new surroundings.

Furnish for less.

Your first impulse when moving into a new place may be to finance a bunch of lovely new furniture to your taste. Don't do it. Spring for the necessities only, and even then look for cheap options—Craigslist and thrift stores.

Use Your social network.

Neighbors, co-workers, and local media are all good resources for saving money. Make friends and get that valuable insider info.

Get lost.

Not totally lost, but look around your city for shops and restaurants that are a bargain. You're more likely to find that $4 falafel place on your own two feet, not in Google Maps.

Move closer to Your needs.

Don't necessarily go for a neighborhood that is close to your friends or hotspots. Try to stay as close as you can to either your job (if it's feasible) or to places like supermarkets, banks, pet stores, and whatever else makes up your weekly errands. You'll save on transportation costs if you can easily walk and bike to where you need to go.

Remember Your deduction.

Bonus tip, if you've moved more than 50 miles from your old location for work reasons, you may qualify for deductible moving expenses. These include cost of packing, cost of storing goods, cost of shipping vehicles, cost of travel and lodging, and more. But consult a tax professional to get the full rundown.

Moving when you're young is exciting and a good step to take—you'll become more independent, worldly, self-sufficient, and hopefully find great opportunities. But it's not a financially simple proposition. As always, planning is your best bet.

Big Moves //
Education

Whether you're going to undergrad, getting a master's degree, or going for that PhD, money is going to play a big role in getting an education. The good news is most students can find funding for their desired education, provided their credit history is clear and their parents' history is good too. The bad news is most of the time it's going to involve loans. Thousands of dollars worth. Nearly 70% of college seniors in 2013 had an average of $28,400 in student loan debt. That's a big hole in your financial life, so here are some tips for making that process less painful.

Paying for School

Decisions, Decisions.

You'll need to weigh the cost of going to school vs. what school you want to attend. Is a private school across the country your best bet? Or is an in-state school going to give you a similar experience for way less debt. Consider whether the reputation of the more expensive school is worth decades of loan payments. Try to make that decision before you even apply.

Borrow Responsibly.

When you are offered aid or loans, don't take all of the money. Only use what you need and consider working part-time while you study, as long as it doesn't affect your grades.

Community College.

Many schools will accept students who have successfully completed their first two years at a community college, possibly saving you thousands while still allowing you to transfer into and graduate from your dream school.

Find Scholarships.

Free money! It's there for the taking, but yes, it involves a lot of applications. In the long run though, it's worth the significant cut to your debt. Merit-based aid and scholarships are your best bet to cover some of the upfront costs of tuition, and sites like Zinch and Fastweb are comprehensive and make them easy to find.

Alternative Credits.

 Credit hours are what you need to earn to get your degree, and your college charges for each and every one. So try to see if your degree program allows you to take cheap summer classes at a community college.

Compare Loans.

 They may be an investment in your future, but you don't need to pick the first one you see. Compare interest rates and repayment terms to get the best deal.

Benefactors.

 AmeriCorps, the Peace Corp, the National Health Services Corps and ROTC programs offer college money in exchange for a service commitment.

Repaying Your Loans

Know Your Loans.

 It's important to keep track of the lender, balance, and repayment status for each of your student loans. These details determine your options for loan repayment and forgiveness. If you're not sure, ask your lender or visit www.nslds.ed.gov.

Know Your Grace Period.

 Different loans have different grace periods. A grace period is how long you can wait after leaving school before you have to make your first payment.

Pick the Right Repayment Option.

 When your federal loans come due, your loan payments will automatically be based on a standard 10-year repayment plan. Extending your repayment period beyond 10 years can lower your monthly payments, but you'll end up paying more interest - often a lot more - over the life of the loan.

Loan Forgiveness.

There are various programs that will forgive all or some of your federal student loans if you work in certain fields or for certain types of employers. Public Service Loan Forgiveness is a federal program that forgives any student debt remaining after 10 years of qualifying payments for people in government, nonprofit, and other public service jobs. Find out more at IBRinfo.org.

Other things to keep in mind are you major, career, and how much you'll likely make after you graduate. That information is readily available from the Bureau of Labor Statistics (http://www.bls.gov/bls/bls-wage.htm) or sites like Glassdoor.com. It's hard to plan out the next few years of your life, but if you have certain aspirations, like living in New York or working in a low-paying industry you love, then keep that in mind before you borrow student loans.

Big Moves //
Self-Employment / Freelance

A mong the many big financial choices you can make is deciding to work for yourself. It has its upsides and downsides, but at some point you thought you'd be better off on your own. Here are some tips to make that crazy transition a little more manageable.

Working for You

Don't do It.

At least weigh the costs. If you currently have a job, you're weighing the freedom and stresses of working independently against paid vacations, pensions, and reliable wages. Is your skillset marketable? Is freelancing common in your industry? Consider all factors before deciding.

Judge the Market.

Are there a lot of people doing what you do? Only a few? Is it in demand? Who are your connections? How much do freelancers usually make in your line of work? Weigh all of those things against your lifestyle and budget.

Willpower.

Do you have the self-control to avoid getting distracted while running your entire business out of a computer? Every second you spend watching cat videos is costing you money.

Advertise Yourself.

Make yourself easy to find and easy to contact. This means being on social media and having a great, well-designed website that advertises what you do and your portfolio. Get on LinkedIn. You may even have to pay someone to set all this up for you.

Cost.

Speaking of a website, you may need to pay someone to do that for you. You may also need to pay for other things your steady job may have otherwise provided, whether it's free equipment or free printer toner. All of these are upfront costs to consider.

Track Your Expenses.

Use an app like Mint to track your spending and see what you spend most by category. It'll keep you motivated and show you where you're lacking or doing well.

Use High-Yield Bank Accounts.

Find checking and savings account with a good interest rate so your money is making more money. Woo! Online banks are generally better in this regard. Schwab and Smartypig are two good options. And while you're add it, find a credit card with good rewards.

Contribute to Retirement.

Set up automatic deductions from your checking account to a retirement account, like an IRA. Try to find a freelancer's union as well, as some offer 401(k) options.

Extra Emergency.

Since a freelancer's job prospects are usually a bit more un-predictable, keep around 6 months worth of pay as a back-up, especially if you decide to switch back into the regular job market and are on the hunt for work.

No Debt.

Don't put yourself in the position of being unemployed on pur-pose and struggling with debt. Clean up your credit health and debts before you decide to jump into being your own boss.

Freelancing is tough, but you can make the process financially eas-ier on yourself by getting your money in order before you embark on the journey. Self-employment takes a lot of smarts and business acumen, but you need to get your credit cards sorted out first.

Big Moves //
Starting a Business

Like freelancing, starting your own business and making it work financially is a scary prospect. As always, we're here to make that easier for you. There's no need to live out the rest of you life wondering of what could have been because of money, we're going to give you the right hacks to live the dream.

Make It Work

Product vs. Service.

If you'd like to start a product-based business, it's going to be harder because it requires higher upfront costs. After all, you need materials to make a product, and those cost money. Start by offering a service related to your idea, and build up the funds you need to make the product-based business happen.

Grind, Grind, Grind.

At some point you'll have to admit that it probably won't pay much to start your own business. You may not even get a paycheck for the first few months (or years). Make sure you're prepared for that reality before you jump in.

Find Funding.

If you're having trouble with money, consider extending your idea into a side business. You may generate more money from it to keep you afloat. And the better you do, the more likely you are to attract investors to your idea.

Get Credit.

Like we said, there may be some upfront costs related to starting your business. Be responsible and keep them to a minimum. Have a backup plan before you grab the credit card.

Incubate!

If you believe you have a solid idea and a workable business plan, you may want to consider a business incubator. Upon acceptance, these programs provide funding designed specifically to financially assist a startup company.

Accelerate!

Like an incubator, they're designed to provide funding. But they expect a quick response to their investment. Only consider it if you're hitting the market fast (and furiously).

Crowdfund.

Kickstarter and other crowdfunding platforms allow the public to invest a small percentage of money in return for a future reward. Make sure to set up your page to be easily understood, widely appealing, and with great rewards.

Those are the basics! It sounds nuts to have to make money to make a business to, well, make money, but that's how it works. You need to be able to fund up front to get the ball rolling. Explore all options before throwing your hands in the air and wondering where the money trees are growing.

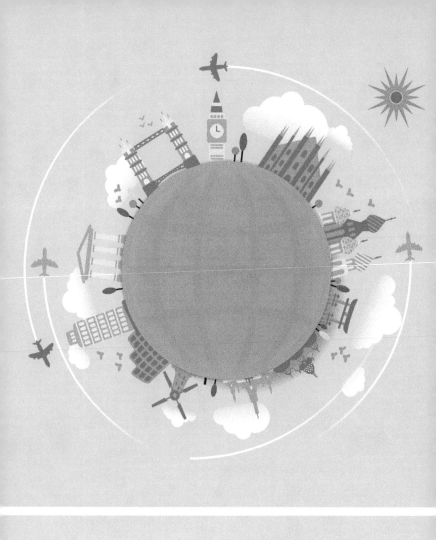

Big Moves //
Around the World

Traveling around the world sounds like an insanely expensive task, but it doesn't have to be. There are plenty of ways to hack the travel industry and make it work for you. You don't have to wait until you retire to make that trip around the world, you just need some good credit and a suitcase.

Up, Up, and Away

Frequent Flyer.

There's a way to earn miles without flying anywhere—credit cards. Choose cards whose rewards are all about earning miles and spend. A lot. But pay them off immediately. You can earn thousands of miles this way, and no one's stopping you.

Special Offers.

Many cards offer a sign up mileage bonus just for opening the account. Or you have to spend a certain amount, a few thousand usually, to get a mileage bonus. To hit the spending limit, use your card for everything. Pre-pay bills if you can. Like we just said though, pay it off.

Get Advice.

There are plenty of people devoted to travel hacking online, so go to sites like FlyerTalk.com to get their insights for your trips and mileage collecting.

Cut Financial Ties.

If your goal is to travel the world, cut as many financial burdens out of your life as possible. It helps if you're not married with kids and have a mortgage. Sell the car, rent with AirBnB instead of leasing, finish school, and go! The only things you should commit to paying for in your travel months are your credit cards, health insurance (very important), and student loans. If you can't get rid of a lease, rent it out on AirBnB in the meantime.

Save or Freelance.

 Unless you're rolling in money, chances are you can't just pick up and stop working for a few months. That is, unless you've saved (noting the themes in this book?). The other option is to telecommute or freelance. If you're already established on this front and have an emergency fund, go for it.

House Sit.

 For cheap accommodations, try housesitting sites. Housecarers.com, Mindmyhouse.com, & Craigslist are all good options.

Be Social.

 There's a reason Facebook and Twitter and every other social network exists, and it's not just to post pictures all day. Use your hopefully vast social resources to find places to crash when you're traveling.

Stay away from Tourist Sites.

 Your best bet when travelling is to live as the locals do. Don't go for the five-star restaurants or travel tours. And plan your activities in advance so you can budget for them properly.

Traveling is probably the best of the experience-related purchases you can make. Those memories don't get outdated, broken, or replaced by new ones. But you can still get them for 50% off.

CHAPTER 5 //
Planning for the Future

**Planning for the Future //
Buying a House**

Your own home! It's what you've always dreamed of—maybe not a white picket fence, but at least your own place with a door and a roof and all that. Buying instead of renting is generally based on whether you'll be getting more bang for your buck for your lifestyle and in your area. **If you choose to buy, here are some tips on the process:**

Start with Your Credit.

 They show whether you are habitually late with payments and whether you've run into any serious credit issues.

Set Your Budget.

 Next, you need to determine how much house you can afford. You can start with an online calculator. For a more accurate figure, ask to be pre-approved by a lender, who will look at your income, debt and credit to determine the kind of loan that's in your league.

Aim within Your Means.

 The rule of thumb is to aim for a home that costs about two-and-a-half times your gross annual salary. If you have significant credit card debt or other financial obligations like alimony or even an expensive hobby, then you may need to set your sights lower.

Line Up Cash.

 You'll need to come up with cash for your down payment and closing costs. Lenders like to see 20% of the home's price as a down payment. If you can put down more than that, the lender may be willing to approve a larger loan. If you have less, you'll need to find loans that can accommodate you.

Find Your Own Agent.

 Most sellers list their homes through an agent -- but those agents work for the seller, not you. They're paid based on a percentage, usually 5 to 7% of the purchase price, so their interest will be in getting you to pay more.

Search for a home.

Your first step here is to figure out what city or neighborhood you want to live in. Look for signs of economic vitality: a mixture of young families and older couples, low unemployment and good incomes.

Consider price.

Try also to get an idea about the real estate market in the area. For example, if homes are selling close to or even above the asking price, that shows the area is desirable. If you have the flexibility, consider doing your house hunt in the off-season -- meaning, generally, the colder months of the year. You'll have less competition and sellers may be more willing to negotiate.

Make an offer.

Once you find the house you want, move quickly to make your bid. If you're working with a buyer's broker, then get advice from him or her on an initial offer. If you're working with a seller's agent, devise the strategy yourself.

Back up the offer.

Try to line up data on at least three houses that have sold recently in the neighborhood. If you really want the house, don't lowball. The seller may give up in disgust. Remember, that your leverage depends on the pace of the market. In a slow market, you've got muscle; in a hot market, you may have none at all.

Secure a Loan.

Now call your mortgage broker or lender and move quickly to agree on terms, if you have not already done so. This is when you decide whether to go with the fixed rate or adjustable rate mortgage and whether to pay points. Expect to pay $50 to $75 for a credit check at this point, and another $150, on average to $300 for an appraisal of the home. Prepare for other fees at closing.

After that, you're almost done! About two days before the actual closing, you will receive a final HUD Settlement Statement from your lender that lists all the charges you can expect to pay at closing. Review it carefully. It will include things like the cost of title insurance that protects you and the lender from any claims someone may make regarding ownership of your property. Congrats, you're officially a homeowner.

Renting Costs

1. **Initial costs** include the rent security deposit and, if applicable, the broker's fee.

2. **Recurring costs** include the monthly rent and the cost of renter's insurance.

3. **Opportunity costs** are calculated each year for both your initial costs and your recurring costs.

4. **Net proceeds** include the return of the rental security deposit, which typically occurs at the end of a lease.

Buying Costs

Initial costs are the costs you incur when you go to the closing for the home you are purchasing. This includes the down payment and other fees.

Recurring costs are expenses you will have to pay monthly or yearly in owning your home. These include mortgage payments, condo fees (or other community living fees), maintenance and renovation costs, property taxes and homeowner's insurance. Property taxes, the interest part of the mortgage payment and, in some cases, a portion of the common charges are tax deductible. The resulting tax savings is accounted for in each item's totals. The mortgage payment amount increases each year for the term of the loan because the tax credit shrinks each year as the interest portion of the payments becomes smaller.

Opportunity costs are tracked for the initial purchase costs and for the recurring costs. The former will give you an idea of how much you could have made if you had invested the down payment instead of buying your home.

Net proceeds is the amount of money you receive from the sale of your home minus the closing costs, which includes the broker's commission and other fees, the remaining principal balance that you pay to your mortgage bank and any tax you have to pay on profit that exceeds your capital gains exclusion. If your total is negative, it means you have done very well: You made enough of a profit that it covered not only the cost of your home, but also all of your recurring expenses.

SAVE
the
DATE

**Planning for the Future //
Marriage and Partnership**

A lot of marriages break up over financial reasons, so it's good to get that out of the way in the first place. Don't let it catch you by surprise. It's easy enough to know if your beloved is a saver or a spender, and you need to have a frank discussion about it. Here are some things to think about before the big day (and hopefully before the engagement):

How to Live Long and Prosper

Your Money Habits.

Start with your own spending behavior. What do you do with money? What has shaped your perspective on it? Do you have discipline or not? What do you need help with? Self-awareness leads to better analysis of your partner.

Observe.

Through conversation and everyday activities, you can begin to see how the person you're dating makes financial decisions. If anything becomes an issue, keep it in mind to discuss.

Talk about Money.

Be frank about money ask you would about sex, hobbies, work, and everything else. Use pop culture whenever possible, it's more fun.

Ask Questions.

If you find it awkward to talk about money habits, admit it. And approach it as a sharing process instead of a judgmental interrogation.

Talk about Debt.

As things get more serious, you need to discuss each other's financial situation. You're marrying this person's finances, so their problems will become your problems.

Compare life goals.

If you want kids, a dog, and a house, but your partner wants to travel the world, those aren't just lifestyle differences. They're extreme examples, but make sure your partner wants the same things you do, and is working toward them as you are (or should be).

Get the paperwork out.

With your financial documents, tally up all your assets — savings, checking, retirement accounts, real estate, collectibles etc., and your debts — school loans, credit card debt, mortgages, etc. Then determine your net worth by subtracting your debts from your assets. At this point, you should also go over your credit reports. And, if you don't know it already, reveal your income to each other.

Set financial goals.

Together. Go for emergency funds (three to six months of essential bills) one- to five-year goals, such as for a down payment or a trip, and then long-term goals such your child's education or retirement. Don't put all your long-term money in retirement accounts, since you won't be able to withdraw it without a penalty.

Set up Your accounts.

You can have all joint accounts, both joint and separate accounts, or separate accounts. Most couples do one of the first two, but if you don't completely trust your partner it's perfectly fine to get a separate account. Though we recommend working out your differences first, but you may never feel comfortable with it, and that's okay,

You'll run into speed bumps along the way in marriage, but preparing for them is the best way to get through them together. That means planning for everything from your unborn kids' college education to how much to lend cousin Jerry when he asks for money. Be completely open with each other and you'll have a leg up on most couples.

**Planning for the Future //
Your Kid, Your Cat, and Your Mom**

D eath isn't something you'd like to prepare for, but it is coming. You're not likely to think about a will until you're older, but consider doing it earlier because, unfortunately, you never know what's going to happen and you probably have more than a few loved ones you'd leave behind. What happens to old Mr. Snowball when you're gone? Prepare for it with a will.

Who Gets Your Stuff

What's a Will?

A will is a document that specifies who will inherit your bank accounts, real estate, jewelry, cars, and other property after you die. You can leave everything to one person or divvy it up in small, specific portions, such as your CD collection to your brother or your sweaters to your best friend

"That sounds Morbid."

It doesn't have to be. You can be weirdly specific and make extravagant demands, or leave everything to the cat. Make it about you. If you don't make a will, then your things will be distributed according to state law.

Prepay the Funeral.

If a will didn't sound morbid, this is, but it's actually something good you can do for your loved ones. They likely would rather mourn you than think about the thousands of dollars it'll cost to bury you. Keep it as part of your emergency fund so your spouse or children can take care of things quickly. You can also prepay it with a company, but make sure to get everything in writing.

Your kids.

For parents, making a will is the single most important thing you can do to make sure your child is cared for by the people you would choose if anything should happen to you and make sure that they have some kind of property to rely on if you're gone.

Charity.

You can leave property to the charities that you support, which is a nice way to think of all that stuff you're not taking with you.

Life insurance and Retirement Accounts.

Keep in mind that whomever you named as beneficiaries when you made these accounts trumps whatever you might say in your will. So call up the company of your IRA or 401(k) and make sure all that information lines up.

You know the old adage about death and taxes. We want to prepare you for both, so take our word for it—it's important.

Planning for the Future //
Retirement

You've made it to your golden years, congrats! Or, more likely, you will someday and you're preparing for it now. Whatever your situation, here are some tips for making sure you have enough once you don't want to work anymore.

The Backup Plan

Use Your 401(k).

If you work for a company that matches your 401(k) contribution, use it! And make sure you're putting in enough for you to get the biggest match. You could get thousands in the long run, all saved up for your old age.

Increase Automatically.

Experts suggest saving enough so that your contribution to the 401(k), plus your company's, add up to a total of 15% of your annual income. But if you don't feel comfortable saving that much just yet, most retirement plans let you set up automatic increases.

Invest.

Put some money from your 401(k) into stocks and some in bonds. If you're in your 20s, invest more in the former. As you get older, move more of your money into bonds, the more conservative option. But give yourself a chance to make money early on.

Keep fees in Mind.

Investing costs a little each year and it's deducted from your investments. Call your company if you're not sure about the fees.

Careful about Quitting.

At most companies, you need to stay for a certain amount of time before your contribution is officially matched. It's called "vesting," and you should take it into considering before quitting your position.

Don't use it Early.

 Don't take money out of your 401(k) before retirement before you can help it. You'll deal with penalty fees. You can, however, move money from an old 401(k) to a new one if you get a new job.

Start Early.

 Like all the other advice we've given about saving, just start as soon as possible. You'll be thankful you did in the long run, because duh, you'll have more money.

The goal of saving for retirement isn't to suck the funds out of your "fun times" allowance, it's to give you a solid backup for when you're tired of working and want to enjoy some years of freedom and downtime. To do that, you'll need over a million dollars at age 59, and where the heck is that coming from? Using all the strategies we've outlined in this book, we think you'll be able to get there, even if it seems far away today.

A NOTE FROM THE AUTHORS

Money matters are sometimes overwhelming, but they don't have to be. These hacks are intended to keep your finances in great shape to help you prepare for future adventures: travel, moving to a new city, buying a home, and more! You can never be too careful about important financial decisions like your credit or your retirement savings. We've done our best to be as thorough as possible in describing all the ups-and-downs you may encounter, but there's always more to learn. After reading this book and checking out your credit report, stay up to date on all your financial options. There's always a great new service or hack to take advantage of. We hope you give our hacks a shot, tweet the ones you love (#MoneyHacks) and write to us @mangomediainc about all your tough financial questions. Good luck with your dollar bills y'all!

DATA SOURCES

http://www.equifax.com/howto/creditreport/images/cpo-slide01.jpg

http://www.marketplace.org/sites/default/files/Credit_report_errors_infographic_0.png

https://c346653.ssl.cf1.rackcdn.com/wp-content/uploads/what-is-a-good-credit-score_lg.jpg

http://visual.ly/eat-seasonably?view=true

http://twocents.lifehacker.com/ask-these-four-questions-to-cut-back-on-unnecessary-sub-1714786196

http://www.business2community.com/infographics/identity-theft-whos-most-at-risk-infographic-0454997

OTHER SOURCES

http://blogs.wsj.com/economics/2014/09/04/it-only-takes-10400-to-be-richer-than-most-millennials/

http://www.dailyfinance.com/2014/09/30/6-money-goals-you-should-conquer-in-your-20s/

http://www.dailyfinance.com/2015/03/05/take-control-today-finances/#!fullscreen&slide=3371340

http://www.gobankingrates.com/personal-finance/20-things-should-saving-money-20s/

http://money.howstuffworks.com/personal-finance/budgeting/savings-accounts1.htm

https://www.mint.com/budgeting-3/the-minimalist-guide-to-budgeting-in-your-20s

http://money.allwomenstalk.com/tips-for-making-a-budget-when-in-your-20s

http://www.nerdwallet.com/blog/credit-card-data/average-credit-card-debt-household/

http://www.practicalmoneyskills.com/personalfinance/creditdebt/cards/terms.php

http://money.usnews.com/money/blogs/my-money/2015/03/26/5-smart-credit-habits-to-start-in-your-20s

https://www.creditkarma.com/article/types-of-credit

https://www.creditkarma.com/article/total-accounts-credit-score

http://www.thepennyhoarder.com/managing-money-in-your-early-20s/

http://www.lifeedited.com/11-steps-for-choosing-the-right-roommate/

http://www.eatingwell.com/healthy_cooking/budget_cooking/12_secrets_to_spending_less_at_the_grocery_store

http://lifehacker.com/are-at-t-and-t-mobiles-frequent-upgrade-plans-worth-it-814398856

http://money.usnews.com/money/blogs/my-money/2013/09/25/7-ways-to-slash-your-cellphone-bill

http://www.shmoop.com/college/save-money-on-your-car.html

http://www.csmonitor.com/Business/Saving-Money/2012/0510/23-ways-to-save-money-on-clothes

http://www.lifehack.org/articles/money/25-apps-that-will-save-you-lots-money.html

https://www.bettermoneyhabits.com/saving-budgeting/saving-for-future/large-purchase.html

http://moneyfor20s.about.com/od/financialrules/bb/largepurchases.htm

http://fusion.net/story/115961/why-doing-taxes-in-your-20s-is-harder-than-you-think/

https://oag.ca.gov/idtheft/facts/top-ten

https://www.fbi.gov/scams-safety/fraud

http://www.csmonitor.com/Business/Saving-Money/2015/0603/Six-ways-to-avoid-apartment-scams-on-Craigslist

http://www.mymovingreviews.com/move/how-to-save-money-in-new-city

http://www.mymovingreviews.com/move/moving-taxes-deduction

http://money.usnews.com/money/blogs/my-money/2013/02/01/4-things-to-consider-before-moving-to-a-new-city

http://www.bankrate.com/finance/college-finance/college-tips/

http://www.forbes.com/pictures/gg45eiefd/1-apply-for-financial-aid/

http://ticas.org/content/posd/top-10-student-loan-tips-recent-graduates

http://www.theguardian.com/money/2011/aug/05/how-to-become-successful-freelance

http://www.forbes.com/sites/laurashin/2014/03/30/how-a-personal-finance-journalist-manages-her-own-money/

http://gizmodo.com/5710654/how-to-fly-35000-miles-visit-4-continents-9-countries-and-15-cities-for-418

http://www.forbes.com/sites/ryanwestwood/2014/10/08/how-to-start-a-business-with-no-money/2/

http://www.vergemagazine.com/travel-intelligence/budget-travel/76-15-ways-to-travel-for-free-or-at-least-cheap.html

http://www.bankrate.com/finance/financial-literacy/why-buy-a-home--1.aspx

http://money.cnn.com/2015/06/08/retirement/401k-guide-millennials/index.html?iid=SF_River

http://time.com/money/3964517/small-business-estate-planning/

http://time.com/money/3916858/paying-off-10000-debt-in-20-months/

http://time.com/money/3938242/millennials-get-out-of-debt/

https://www.fdic.gov/deposit/deposits/brochures/your_insured_deposits-english.html

https://www.annualcreditreport.com/index.action